MW00878823

When I walked in the door at Caterpillar in 1976, retirement was not a hot topic in my life. My dad was a business owner, and at age 65, he had no plans or desires to retire. In fact, he feared retirement.

While saving was instilled in me at a young age, I adopted the "squirrel method" for financial planning. I buried as many nuts on the way home and made sure they were in a safe place.

In college, life insurance had been negatively flavored by piranhas who preyed on college seniors. It didn't take long at Caterpillar to hear about stock plans and why they were the key to retirement. Stock plans turned into IRAs and then 401(k)s. Once again, the older leaders and supervisors at work provided their takes on financial planning. As it happened, I did find a Northwestern Mutual advisor when children and house loans entered my life, which led me to purchase some life insurance coverage.

Yet, truth be told, I still did not give financial planning any serious consideration—except to save as much as I could, ask what investments colleagues were selecting in their 401(k)s, and read a few books.

It wasn't until I had grandchildren when I overheard Josh Waite in discussion with another person at the local gym. I heard the name Northwestern Mutual mentioned, which I knew had a great reputation. I immediately introduced myself and asked if he could review my old insurance plans. That random exchange, which I believe today was all a part of God's plan, was the beginning of a relationship with Josh that is now approaching fifteen years.

In meeting Josh, I was drawn to his discipline in all areas of his life—especially how he approached my wife, my family, and my interests, plans, and desires with empathy and care. He offered up choices that I had not imagined nor knew existed within Caterpillar's retirement system, as I had thought I was too far away from retirement to consider them. And with his help, we were able to leverage all the decisions we had made over time to retire early and make possible for my wife and I to transition to a new phase of life in which we enjoy impacting other's lives and giving back what God has blessed us with.

As I've told many colleagues and friends who asked about my retirement plans and decisions to retire, it all comes down to trust. You either trust yourself and your abilities, or you trust someone who has character, skills, and discipline to guide you. Josh exemplifies someone you can trust, and his book is a great resource as you take your journey up and down the mountain.

— Ed Brockway, Machine Products Manager, Defense and Federal Products, Caterpillar Inc.

As I read Josh Waite's words, I found myself both reflecting on the journey I have been on with him these past many years, as well as realizing both the personal commitment and passion he has for the work he does with his clients every day.

The analogy he uses in his introduction to climbing Mount Rainier resonated with me the moment I read it, and I reflected on this analogy multiple times while reading the rest of his book. As a corporate professional, I found myself always looking "up" ... for the next achievement, the next career advancement, always pushing for success and accomplishments. Only once I reached the "top of the mountain" did I give a moment's thought to the next leg of the journey, which was retirement. Prior to that, things were happening so fast, due to many external influences, that I didn't have much time to ponder my choices: Deadlines were given, and decisions had to be made.

The landscape was uncertain, slick and icy for sure, and my footing was not firm. Beyond that, by then, I was fatigued from all the exertion it took to get to "the top" and to hold my place there successfully.

My peace of mind came from knowing that the many years of following Josh's map had prepared me for this moment more than I had realized. While I executed on the things he recommended to me over time, I will admit I didn't always take the time to monitor the progress of those investments. I had confidence that Josh and his team were doing it for me, much like the Sherpas who guide the climbers up and down Mount Rainier.

Consulting with Josh during this time of critical decision gave me the confidence that I could take this leap. I was prepared, and I could in fact retire earlier than many thought I would!

To give perspective, I began my career with Caterpillar as a "mid-career hire," having worked for another Fortune 100 company for eleven years. My decision to make a career move was based on several of the truths Josh lists in Chapter 1: I was devoted to my family and extremely committed to my career and wanted a solid financial future that allowed me to do the things in life that were important to me.

I entered Caterpillar in 1989, and took a considerable step backward in my career, both financially and in my position, which I have never regretted. My commitment to my family prohibited me from considering some opportunities in the initial stages of my career, as I wanted to remain in the Peoria area until my son went off to college.

In the late 1990s, I began once again to find myself driving my career forward and upward. Opportunities were plentiful, if you were willing to make the sacrifices required. The next fifteen (plus) years of my career provided expanded scope of responsibilities around the globe, ever increasing travel, extended work hours and even living in Asia, none of which I regret.

Upon retirement, I held the position of global responsibility for the largest wholly owned subsidiary of Caterpillar.

Thank goodness, I was being guided by Josh early on, making the investments, as hard as they were at first, toward the future I knew I wanted. Regardless of where I lived, what time zone I was in, Josh always kept in touch to give me updates, make new recommendations, and often provide me simplified guidance on the ever-increasing complex company benefits and financial decisions I needed to make. He created the road map, based on the ever-changing options and goals that I had.

Yet, to do so as successfully as he has, I had to trust him. He had to be given very personal information, not only about my finances, but also my values, goals and yes, maybe even some of my fears and past failures.

Finding the right person that you can feel confident and comfortable with is probably the single most difficult hurdle to overcome. This book provides some good advice and structure to making that selection in Chapter 3.

The Financial Security Checklist is very valuable in helping you prioritize your financial needs and create that map to success. We are all different and our paths will vary, but having a guide helps us make those decisions. This book provides the step-by-step insight and guidance that explains those steps, so you can evaluate them easily.

Even in retirement, I need to consult with Josh and his team regularly. Things are constantly changing. Josh still challenges me to consider the next level of investment or alternative routes on the map to take.

My advice to you is: Begin your planning NOW. It is never too early! Using this road map and the team of experts available to you from Josh's organization will help you do so with no pressure. They are truly here to give you guidance, answer your questions in this ever-complex arena and take as much of the burden off of you as possible, so you can focus on the other priorities in your life.

I wish you much success in life.

— *Kathy Mock, Former VP, Global Human Resources, Solar Turbines Incorporated, a Caterpillar Company*

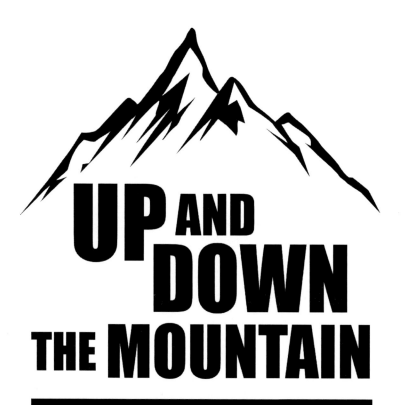

UP AND DOWN THE MOUNTAIN

Financial Planning for Fortune 500 Executives

JOSHUA T. WAITE

Up and Down the Mountain: Financial Planning for Fortune 500 Executives

This is dedicated to Dad and Grandma Carol:

Two of my heroes in life who continue to teach me how to be a better person as they look down from Heaven.

FOREWORD

IT IS A PRIVILEGE TO BE ASKED to write a foreword for this important book. This is essentially my story: I am the fortunate recipient of the coaching and council as provided by Josh and his team. This advice has provided me peace of mind with my financial plan that I would not have enjoyed without knowing him.

Far more importantly, the work I have done over several years with Josh enabled me to care for my family and my wife as she battled and died from cancer. Josh's team helped me make better financial decisions while working, and to then be in a position to retire early from a corporate career. This was a goal I expressed to Josh in one our first conversations—and he listened.

In fact, he listens more than he speaks, which is a good characteristic for an adviser.

Everyone has unique circumstances, and, in my case, I needed a plan that would enable me to live well with my wife and support her as she battled cancer. We knew from her prognosis that she would likely die before I would, and I wanted a financial plan that would enable us enjoy life while she was here, and one that would enable me to care for her full-time should she need me.

We were able to do that, and I am extremely grateful for the opportunity this has afforded me.

I met Josh after a positive referral from a good friend of mine. We began informal discussions shortly after the 2009 market crash. Two realities were weighing on my mind at that point: First, I knew I needed a comprehensive financial plan to care for my family. Secondly, I knew the realities of corporate life. I wanted to be able to leave the company when I needed to care for my wife, rather than when the company decided they no longer needed me.

Please don't misunderstand me on this point: I absolutely loved my career with Caterpillar, and I cannot think of a better organization with which to work. However, the crash of 2009 emphasized the realities of business decisions, and I needed a plan.

As life events transpired, I needed to retire in late 2015. I had a plan, and I was ready.

I encourage you to read Josh's guidelines and consider his approach. As a successful engineer and businessman I entered our relationship skeptically. I thought, *Hey, I'm a smart guy. I read financial planning material. I can do this!*

While I *could* do this, the truth is that I had not and did not. I procrastinated.

Further, the highest value Josh and his team offer is not in any specific ideas they bring forward, rather, it is their council and discussion. They know many things that I do not, but the two most important elements are:

1. Detailed knowledge of the financial benefits available to executives; and
2. A much broader perspective on life events and potential pitfalls and opportunities...a far bigger horizon.

These elements have tremendous value, and combined with a no-pressure approach, I looked forward to my discussions with Josh and his team in the past, and I continue to benefit from their council today.

Best of luck with your own financial planning process, but I think you need more than luck! You need a plan.

> — *Reid Waitt, Former General Manager of the Compact Construction Equipment Business for Caterpillar's Building Construction Products Division*

TABLE OF CONTENTS

TABLE OF CONTENTS

INTRODUCTION

IN 2015, MY BROTHER, SISTER, and I decided to climb Mount Rainier. My sister, Ellie, had moved to Seattle a few years earlier. Always the adventurer, she recruited my brother and I to climb one of the tallest mountains in the United States, 14,411 feet above sea level.

As it happened, 2015 was the ten-year anniversary of us siblings running the Chicago marathon together, which we had done to raise money and as a memorial for our dad, who had died from cancer the year prior. To plan, train, and get together to climb the highest mountain in Washington seemed like another fitting tribute for our dad. He was passionate about family time and relationship-building.

I had never done anything like that climb. I had never even been a serious hiker, much less climbed a mountain. To prepare, I started doing some research on mountain climbing and learned several things: One statistic that surprised me was that most accidents, and certainly most fatalities, do not happen on the way up the mountain. They happen on the way down.

As I climbed Mount Rainier, I suddenly understood why this statistic was true. For one thing, most of the mountain is a glacier. Hikes usually begin in the middle of the night, or early morning, when the ice is frozen hard. By mid-morning, hikers reach the summit, and as they begin their descent in late morning or early afternoon, that top layer of ice has started to melt with the sun, leaving a slick and often slushy surface. A hiker's footing is not as stable on the way down a mountain.

Beyond that, and true of all mountains, whether they are covered in glaciers or not, is this: On the way down, you are physically fatigued from all the exertion.

The mental fatigue is even more extreme.

When I ran the Chicago Marathon, I was done when I crossed the finish line. I did not have anywhere else to go, so I literally lay on my back on the streets of Chicago for a while. I was filled with adrenaline, pride, and a lot of emotion, so I took my time. I got up when I decided to get up.

I had a similar rush of adrenaline and emotion when I stood on the top of Mount Rainier with my brother and my sister. The difference was this: In this instance, we were allowed to linger only for about fifteen minutes to take pictures. But then, we had to turn around and head down the mountain, which was a seven-hour trek. The mental exhaustion of reaching that high, but being unable to lay down and relax, made coming down much, much more challenging than the trip to the top.

I think of this story often in my career because it is a great analogy to retirement planning. We focus most of our time thinking about how to get to the top of the mountain—how to get to retirement. But the truth is, planning is often more challenging on the way down than on the way up because we assume we have "made it," when, in a lot of ways, the journey has just begun. My goal, then, as a financial planner is to help people live life differently. In fact, this is my mission statement. I want my clients to think differently about their planning. In doing so, I believe they will lead more joyful, rewarding lives today as a result of the peace of mind they have knowing their plan is secure for the future.

The way up the mountain is straightforward: save enough money. The strategy, while not easy to execute, is not all that complicated. It is hard to screw things up if you save enough.

Getting down the mountain, or transitioning into the distribution phase of planning, is where most of the mistakes happen. The false expectation that retirement is an easy downhill trip can blind people to their need for a guide and a map for this critical stage of their journey. The work we do with clients helps them plan ahead and avoid the pitfalls and slippery slopes during the retirement years.

So what were the keys to a three-day trip, up and down Mount Rainier, with no accidents, no injuries, and no fatalities? And how does that apply to retirement planning? Two key variables give you the answers:

1. WE HAD A MAP.

That map gave us the best path we should take to get up the mountain, and then, most importantly, the best path to descend. Ours was not the only path. Some were more difficult, for more experienced hikers. One route required navigating crevasses or steep cliffs with ropes and pulleys. We did not take that route.

The route we took was incredibly steep, which meant we were on switchback paths for hours. This might have seemed tedious at times, but it was the right path for us because of our ability and training. And we had the map as our guide.

The map was essential in choosing which path we should take, and I compare that to a financial plan. If you do not have a financial plan, you will face challenges in knowing which route to go. If you start coming down the mountain and you choose the wrong path, you cannot go back up and choose a different route. You are stuck on the path that you are on. With a retirement plan, some of the decisions you make at the start are irrevocable. For example, once you start unwinding certain investments, you cannot go back and change your mind.

2.   WE HAD GUIDES.

This was perhaps more important than having a map. Our guides were experienced climbers who knew Mount Rainier well. Each guide was assigned two climbers to help. These guides added something I could not have provided, and they were as essential—if not more—as our good maps.

The difference they made in our journey was not because they were smarter than the rest of us. Intelligence and IQ did not matter, nor did physical condition. Exercise, health, and fitness are priorities for me, and our guides were not in better physical condition than I was. After all, they were not pulling us up and down the mountain! We had trained extensively for this.

So, if they were not smarter and they were not in better shape, what was it they brought to the table?

It was perspective—the perspective that comes with experience. They had navigated up and down Mount Rainier hundreds of times. It was their job and their passion. That perspective was incredibly valuable at certain points along the journey.

That same perspective is what we bring to the table with our clients, helping them see things they would otherwise miss. We know what routes are best and what pitfalls to avoid. We have helped hundreds of people navigate the crevasses of taxes, shortfalls, and gaps so they can live life differently and have peace of mind in their retirement years.

If you need help up and down your financial planning "mountain," please contact me at joshwaite@upanddownthemountain.com.

UP AND DOWN THE MOUNTAIN

Our team, climbers, and guides at the summit of Mount Rainier.

My sister, Ellie, and my brother, Zach, capturing the moment with me at the summit.

CHAPTER ONE

MY MISSION

MY MISSION IN LIFE AND as a financial advisor is to help those I lead live life differently. Different means developing a financial plan, as most people do not make the time to be intentional. Different means charting a course with focused planning and follow-through, as many people who create a plan need help staying on course. Different mean living life with the security and contentment that comes when a plan is in place.

After years of living out this mission in daily interactions with my clients, many truths have become quite clear. These truths are my motivation for writing this book.

TRUTH #1:

MY CLIENTS ARE EXTREMELY COMMITTED TO THEIR CAREERS

While I work with many individuals across different industries and in every level of the organizations, my main focus has been with executives of Caterpillar, Inc.[1] I have rarely seen a higher commitment level or intensity of focus than

---

1   I am not endorsed by nor affiliated with Caterpillar, Inc.

that of manager or executive. There is simply no chance of becoming a manager or executive in a high-performance company without this intensity.

TRUTH #2:

MY CLIENTS HAVE A DEEP LOVE FOR THEIR FAMILIES.

A stereotype exists of the busy executive who neglects his or her family, but I have not noticed this to be true. I have noticed that the intensity brought to an executive's careers does not take the place of commitment to family. Rather, commitment to family is usually the motivating factor that allows a person to reach executive-status. Watching this commitment is one of the joys of my career, as I get to spend time every day with family-oriented individuals who care more about others than themselves and have clear values and priorities.

TRUTH #3:

MY CLIENTS HAVE FULL LIVES WITH RICH AND VARIED INTERESTS.

Most professionals have interests and hobbies outside of their family and professional lives. When they can carve out the time, my clients tell me they want the ability to fully enjoy their interests, which includes church, sports, and giving back in the community.

TRUTH #4:

MY CLIENTS CONSIDER TIME A PRECIOUS COMMODITY AND WANT A SOLID FINANCIAL PLAN.

Your professional life commands much time and intensity. Your love and commitment to family takes more time. Your hobbies and interests fill the precious little cracks of time that are left. Your available time remaining to develop and maintain a financial plan is quite limited.

This is why so many executives at Caterpillar Inc. partner with me: They can appropriately address this area of their life, but they can still preserve their free time doing things they love.

Speaking personally, my priorities are faith, family, fitness, and career—in that order. Finding time for my own personal financial planning is often a challenge, even though it is what I do for a living. As is so often the case in life, I am just as guilty as the next person in putting the urgent, though often unimportant, in front of what is important but can be neglected. I have heard it said, most families spend more time planning their summer vacation each year than they do planning for their financial future. If this describes you, you are not alone.

Frankly, the system is stacked against most individuals. They would need a degree in finance just to understand the structures and lingo. As a result, most people lack confidence in

> # MY MISSION IS TO HELP THOSE I LEAD LIVE LIFE DIFFERENTLY.

their financial decisions. They do not plan to fail. They simply fail to plan.

After many years of watching good people fall into this trap, I decided to create a straightforward, easy-to-understand reference manual to help people start their journey toward the financial security that arises from a solid plan implemented by a strong team. This book is about our fictional client "Carol," who can show you what it is like to work with our firm and achieve your dream of financial security so that you can live life differently.

CHAPTER TWO

THE PROBLEM

MEET CAROL. AT THE AGE OF 50, Carol appears to have it all together. A traditional Midwesterner, she is committed to her religious affiliation, intentionally engaged in the lives of her family, and passionately involved in several local charities.

From a financial perspective, Carol is usually conservative, and she is inclined to save versus spend. Over the years, she has built a successful career climbing the corporate ladder at the local Fortune 500 corporation. She began her career right out of college with an engineering degree from a Big Ten university, and she has taken her initial technical knowledge to grow into an effective manager, leading a team of many direct reports.

As part of her career path, Carol has been asked to move her family many times across the country, and once internationally. While she feels fairly settled today, Carol knows that her company expects her to travel every other month to meet with members of her team and oversee certain facilities.

In addition to her career, Carol places a high priority

on time with her family. Carol is married to her high school sweetheart, Walter, and has raised two children, Ben and Ava, who are quickly becoming teenagers.

Sound somewhat familiar?

Carol has one big problem: Life has become too chaotic to create, implement, monitor, or maintain a financial plan without the help of a financial planning team. Her company has changed its benefits package many times over the last five years. Her job and her family take precedence over attempting to understand the new benefit changes that are detailed in an email buried somewhere in her inbox.

She sees retirement looming in the distance and it seems closer than ever before. She is nagged by doubt and worry that she and Walter are not doing everything they can to prepare. She wonders if she is maximizing all the benefits her company offers.

While all the information is technically "at her fingertips" on the company website, she simply has no time available to search, read, and investigate the impact of the latest change on her personal financial picture. While the intentions are good, her Human Resource Department essentially has its hands tied when it comes to giving advice. It could be putting the company at legal risk by providing Carol with specific financial advice. Often, the HR Department does not even have the knowledge or credentials to fully assist her.

When she has asked HR for help in the past, the department usually points her back to the company website and those "benefits updates" emails buried in her inbox.

When she carves out the time on her calendar and attempts to get caught up on all the information related to her benefit package, Carol faces another challenge: a language barrier. Financial concepts and terminology often seem like a foreign language. They certainly do not make for light reading.

This is the problem many executives face today. Financial resources, intelligence, and information are not the barriers to living life differently through a solid financial plan. The problems are lack of time and lack of clear guidance needed to develop a simple, detailed roadmap to attain financial security and peace of mind.

It is no surprise, then, that the most common response our team receives after working with individuals like Carol is this: "I would have never known this was available unless you had mentioned it and made sense of it."

Our team's goal is to make sure that our Caterpillar clients are fully aware of the resources available through both their company benefit packages and outside providers. We research and investigate details of the company benefits package, identify gaps we need to plug and opportunities to maximize, run the models, crunch the numbers, and come up with the best, simplified options that help our clients reach their goals and dreams of financial security.

Through the simple concepts described in the following chapters, we hope to help you, like Carol, live life differently by creating your path to financial security.

CHAPTER THREE

SELECTING A FINANCIAL ADVISOR

ENLISTING THE HELP OF A relative stranger to navigate the financial mountains of one's life can be an intimidating assignment. A financial advisor can best help if Carol can be open and share her hopes, dreams, failures, successes, and, most certainly, her current financial picture.

Scary? It certainly can be. Assuming she picks a good one, her financial advisor would know more about her deepest dreams, her values, and her goals than most people in her life. The first and most important step in Carol's pursuit of reaching financial security, then, is selecting an advisor.

EXPERIENCE

A benefit package for someone at Carol's level in her organization is complex, and it requires an advisor with years of experience in the industry, and preferably with a history of working with her company's benefit packages.

And here is something else to consider: Financial services is a high-turnover industry, something I know about firsthand, not only as a wealth management advisor with my own personal practice, but also in my role as managing director of our office where I recruit, coach, and mentor new financial representatives and advisors.

Carol should look for an advisor with a track record. Five is the magic number here. Carol should know that in the financial services industry, if an advisor has made it past the five-year mark, the advisor has a much higher likelihood of staying power. This is important because Carol will want an advisor who can be there for her as she retires and needs help down the mountain.

For Carol to avoid feeling like she is going through a revolving door of financial advisors, she should do her due diligence so that she can develop a stable, durable plan that sees her through retirement and beyond, without the constant need to start over and, once again, divulge her personal dreams, goals, and financial means.

CREDENTIALS

Carol should also evaluate the advisor's credentials and designations. Designations and credentials in the financial planning industry show a commitment to one's practice and profession. They indicate advisors who have taken the initiative, often on their own and at their personal expense, to further educate themselves. Those abbreviations that follow an advisor's name—like CFP®, CFA®, CLU®, and ChFC®—indicate that the advisor is in this career for the long haul and is intent on becoming an expert, which resonates with an engineer like Carol.

To use an analogy from the medical field, Carol certainly would not choose a surgeon for a life-threatening procedure without checking to make sure the physician had completed all his or her appropriate training. That is not exactly a fair analogy since it is illegal to practice medicine without the appropriate training and license. In the finance industry, however, training and experience can vary greatly. Financial advisors throughout the country are offering financial advice without having any further training or education outside of their firm's basic orientation.

The most credible and widely recognized industry designations Carol should look for include CERTIFIED FINANCIAL PLANNER™ (CFP®) professional, Chartered Financial Analyst (CFA®), Chartered Life Underwriter (CLU®), and Chartered Financial Consultant (ChFC®). If Carol meets someone who does not have one of these designations, she can and should ask why. The advisor should have a good explanation that includes his or her current study plan. As with other professional career paths, education is essential to developing the expertise to provide the very best counsel possible.

SPECIALIZED KNOWLEDGE

Finally, Carol should consider working with an advisor or advisory team that has experience and specialized knowledge of her company's compensation and benefit plans. While many Fortune 500 companies share similar benefit package features, each one has its unique nuances that could be missed if the advisor does not work regularly with other executives at the same company. My niche is Caterpillar Inc. executives. Working with this group for many years allows us to have very specific knowledge and insight into their benefits and the best way to maximize them. A team committed to providing expert advice and service, with a specific knowledge of Caterpillar, is essential.

CHAPTER FOUR

PRIORITIZING FINANCIAL NEEDS AND OBJECTIVES

NOW THAT CAROL HAS CHOSEN a financial advisor, the next question she should ask is, "How should I go about prioritizing my different goals and objectives?"

She has been saving for retirement, but hasn't considered disability insurance. She has money for college, but does not have an emergency fund. She knows it is important to have a will and trust in place, but she has not reviewed her current investment allocation in her 401(k). Knowing what her goals are, and then knowing what needs to be done first, are two completely different things.

When it comes to prioritizing Carol's goals and objectives, it could be easy to mistakenly start in the wrong place, and therefore, open her plans up to risks that could have been avoided. And too often, individuals just like Carol make that very mistake.

Our team would suggest she follow a process that is largely endorsed by the financial planning industry, and one that we have found to be successful in achieving one's goals while mitigating risk. This illustration depicts how Carol should prioritize building her financial plan.

Let us use the analogy of building a home. For a solid financial plan, you start with the foundation and build your way up. After all, you would not start framing walls before pouring a foundation. In financial planning, that foundation for Carol starts with protecting against risks that could collapse or demolish her plans and dreams for her family. These risks include:

- Becoming sick or hurt and unable to work,
- Unexpectedly passing away,
- The inability to care for oneself at later stages of life
- Emergency expenses.

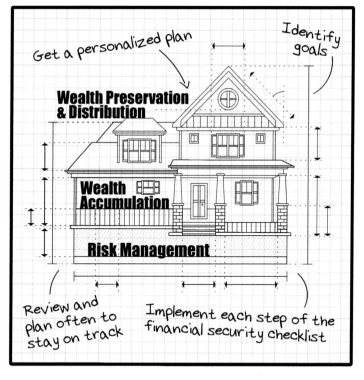

By addressing her risks first, she then has a solid foundation to build upon as she moves toward accumulating wealth. Risk assessment may be uncomfortable to think about, but is essential to address early.

The wealth accumulation phase is often the more exciting phase. With the foundation laid, the building begins to take shape. In the wealth accumulation phase, she will begin saving and investing toward retirement, her children's education, and future major purchases like buying a home, or buying a second home. Assuming she is successful over her lifetime in the wealth accumulation phase, she will then turn her focus to preserving and distributing that wealth to the people and organizations she cares about.

Our team's real-life experience suggests that most individuals like Carol would much prefer to discuss ideas about accumulating wealth through saving and investing, as opposed to addressing the risks of something going wrong. Frankly, this preference makes sense to me, at least emotionally. Who wouldn't rather talk about accumulating wealth and seeing their net worth grow, envisioning vacations and a second home, versus having the uncomfortable conversation regarding what would happen if they didn't make it home that night?

But assume for a second that Carol's financial advisor does just that. He allows Carol's emotional preference to come first and establishes an investment account before she addresses the financial risk she and her family are facing. The advisor sets up an investment account for her initially, for example saving $1,000 a month into a 529 College Savings Plan, and postpones discussing the shortage in her life insurance planning.

God forbid Carol passes away prior to having the follow up conversation about her insurance planning. How good of a job would her financial advisor have done for Carol and her family? I would suggest a poor one.

If you think about it, whatever had been saved up until that point in the 529 Plan would pale in comparison to the money needed to replace her lost income, and provide for her family in the manner she had intended. The 529 Plan would likely need to be liquidated (incurring possible fees and tax penalties) just to help cover some of the now more important needs of the family.

Hopefully, you see the logic. A solid financial plan starts with protecting Carol's risks, and looks ahead to her wealth accumulation and even beyond to the legacy years where she can preserve and distribute wealth according to her goals and values. When working with Caterpillar executives, we use the following checklist to ensure all our clients' priorities are addressed, and addressed in the appropriate order.

FINANCIAL SECURITY CHECKLIST

- ☐ **Step 1:** Comprehensive financial plan
- ☐ **Step 2:** Protect income (disability insurance)
- ☐ **Step 3:** Adequate life insurance (both spouses)
- ☐ **Step 4:** Estate planning
  (wills, trust, durable/living powers of attorney)
- ☐ **Step 5:** Emergency fund
  (three to six months of expenses)
- ☐ **Step 6:** Debt reduction
- ☐ **Step 7:** Retirement planning
- ☐ **Step 8:** Long-term care planning
- ☐ **Step 9:** Education funding

OTHER CONSIDERATIONS:

- ☐ Life insurance for children/grandchildren
  (guarantee insurability)
- ☐ Save twenty percent of income long-term
- ☐ Liability umbrella ($1,000,000 minimum)
- ☐ Executed wealth-management philosophy
  (asset allocation, asset location, cash reserve)
- ☐ Team of experts (CFP®, CPA, JD, banker/
  mortgage professional, insurance agent)
- ☐ Annual review

This is the checklist we will use throughout the remainder
of this book to address Carol's financial planning needs.

CHAPTER FIVE

STEP ①

THE FINANCIAL PLAN

REGARDING THIS FINANCIAL HOUSE that Carol is building, consider that a step comes even before laying the foundation. Can you guess it? How about meeting with an architect and contractor to create a formal plan and a set of blueprints? A person building her home does not just start digging the foundation and framing up walls before spending adequate time thinking through all the possibilities on how to best design a house to meet one's needs as a family. Financial planning is no different.

Or, at least, it shouldn't be.

Over the years, I have met with many potential clients who told me they already had an advisor. But after meeting with them and taking them through our planning process, these clients often realized that they had a few financial products, like investment accounts and insurance policies. Essentially, they had some nice window treatments.

What they **did not have** was a financial plan.

Why is this significant? First, recent surveys suggest seventy percent of Americans want a financial plan, but only thirty percent have one.[2] People like Carol want a plan, a roadmap, or a blueprint to direct them to accomplish their goals. But what they get from many financial advisors are solutions, products, and a sales pitch.

This is not to say the solutions and products are not important. They certainly are important, but they should be implemented in the context of an overall financial plan. The plan should drive what products are implemented, and not the other way around.

If Carol's financial advisor is not spending time actively listening and attempting to truly understand her family's goals and dreams first, she does not have a true advisor. She has a salesperson. The plan has to come first, otherwise, how would the advisor know what to recommend? Therefore, after she has selected a financial advisor, Step 1 on Carol's Financial Security Checklist is to work with her advisor to create a comprehensive financial plan.

---

2   Northwestern Mutual 2016 Planning and Progress Study- Assessing Financial Security," [Online]. Available: https://www.northwesternmutual.com/about-us/studies/planning-and-progress-study-2016.

CHAPTER SIX

STEP 2

DISABILITY INSURANCE

ONCE CAROL HAS AN ADVISOR, and that advisor has helped her complete a comprehensive plan, Carol can begin addressing the risk management portion of her financial plan. The top priority in this area, and Step 2 on the Financial Security Checklist, will be protecting her family against the risk of sickness or injury. Prior to the real estate bubble in 2008 and 2009, becoming disabled and unable to work was the number-one reason for home foreclosure.[3] Consider also that we are twice as likely to become disabled prior to age 65 than we are to die prematurely.[4,5]

---

3   C. T. a. E. R. a. H. M. Robertson, "Get Sick, Get Out: The Medical Causes of Home Mortgage Foreclosures," Health Matrix: Journal of Law-Medicine, vol. 18, no. 65, p. Available at SSRN: https://ssrn.com/abs, 2008.

4   S. o. A. I. D. E. C. 1. P. Table and S. o. A. 2. V. Table, "https://www.soa.org," 1999, 2001. [Online]. Available: https://www.google.com/search?source=hp&q=Table%2C+Society+of+Actuaries+Individual+Disability+Experience+Committee+1999+Preliminary%3B+Table%2C+Society+of+Actuaries+2001+Valuation&oq=Table%2C+Society+of+Actuaries+Individual+Disability+Experience+Committee. [Accessed 20 September 2017].

5   Nothwestern Mutual for Forbes BrandVoice, "www. Forbes.com," 4 June 2013. [Online]. Available: https://www.forbes.com/sites/northwesternmutual/2013/06/04/in-a-changing-economy-protect-your-most-valuable-asset-income/#2bf299bf52cd. [Accessed 20 September 2017].

Likelihood of Long-Term Disability vs. Death Before Age 65

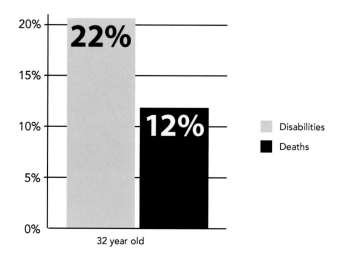

Source: Society of Actuaries Individual Disability Experience Committee 1999 Preliminary Table;
Society of Actuaries 2001 Valuation Basic Table

If Carol starts to quantify what she is protecting, she will see that her future earning potential is by far her largest financial asset. If she works for ten more years, her $200,000 salary will likely grow to $296,000 at retirement, meaning Carol will earn a total of at least 2.4 million over the next decade. Almost every other financial goal she shares with her financial advisor hinges on her having income coming in the door each month to fund the goal. Her goals of education funding, retirement planning, and debt reduction, will crumble with a disability that sharply reduces her income. In other words, Carol's income is something she simply cannot afford to lose.

So why has Carol, like many of her peers, never addressed a risk that could derail all her careful plans? Consider starting this conversation: "Honey, what would we do if you weren't able to work tomorrow?"

Who wants to start dinner conversation with this question? Few people bring this up to their spouses. Beyond that disability insurance is not as widely talked about in the media as life, home, and auto insurance. To make matters worse, even if Carol was already working with a financial advisor, many advisors do not truly understand the many intricacies of disability insurance, and the advisors themselves choose not to bring the topic up with their clients (which I think is a big mistake!).

While each company's benefits package is going to differ slightly, most Fortune 500 companies offer similar benefits. Through her employer, Carol has both short-term

INSURE AGAINST THE THINGS YOU CANNOT AFFORD TO LOSE

and long-term group disability insurance. Her short-term disability benefit provides coverage up to one hundred percent of her base pay for eight weeks, and then seventy percent of base pay in weeks nine through twenty-six. Her long-term disability benefit pays her sixty-five percent of her usual base pay and continues until she reaches age sixty-five. This means that in the event of disability, for the first eight weeks, Carol will receive the same paycheck she had been making while healthy and working. Then, for the next seventeen weeks, Carol will receive seventy percent of what she had been making while healthy and working. In other words, she will have a thirty percent pay cut.

Once the short-term disability coverage has expired at the end of week twenty-six, Carol's long-term disability coverage then kicks in. At that point, assuming she continues to be unable to work, she would continue to receive sixty-five percent of her base pay compensation until she reaches age sixty-five.

The question Carol should ask herself is, "How would it affect my family financially if I were to take a thirty-five percent pay cut?"

When I ask clients this question, I often get answers like,

- "We would be in big trouble!"
- "That would hurt," or
- Some more colorful version of that answer.

Suffice it to say, most people do not have a thirty-five percent cushion of unallocated, unnecessary resources that could easily be done away with.

Carol should also consider a couple of other additional points regarding this coverage. First, because her benefit is a group plan, meaning her employer is providing it to all employees, it is a free benefit with no cost to her. While this is a plus on the surface, it comes at a cost. If she becomes disabled, the sixty-five percent benefit that she receives will still be treated as taxable income. This means she will pay ordinary income taxes on it. In other words, given that Carol's tax rate is 35 percent, she will take a thirty-five percent pay cut on her **after-tax pay**, something she might not have fully understood without the guidance of an advisor with deep understanding of her company's benefits package.

Second, the sixty-five percent benefit is determined by her base salary. It does not take into consideration any pay such as bonuses, restricted stock or stock options. Such pay is considered "at risk" because it is based on company profits and not guaranteed, so employer-provided disability coverage does not include it.

For Carol, and many of our clients, this is increasingly problematic. With each promotion Carol receives, the greater percentage of her total compensation is tied to "at risk" pay. For example, we have clients whose base salary is only forty percent of their total compensation. This means that after taxes, they would take a sixty percent pay cut!

Finally, other parts of Carol's total compensation package such as pension, 401(k), and medical benefits may be affected as well.

And if that is not enough, her company's group long-term disability insurance has a limited definition of what it takes to actually qualify for the disability coverage. Remember, disability insurance is a legal contract written by attorneys at an insurance company and administered in accordance with the contract's terms. It is very important to be aware that whether or not you collect is primarily determined by how the insurance contract reads.

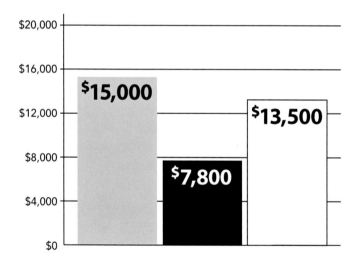

Monthly Take Home Pay/Benefit/Coverage

Source: Society of Actuaries Individual Disability Experience Committee 1999 Preliminary Table;
Society of Actuaries 2001 Valuation Basic Table

In Carol's case, the contract is fairly typical and states that in order for her to be considered disabled, she would need to be unable to do practically anything. The specific language reads, "If one is able to do **anything** your education, training, or experience qualifies you to do, you are **not** disabled".

As an engineer by training, Carol has the education, training, and experience to do a lot of things, and may not collect any benefits under the company's group plan definition if she can use those skills to do another job, even a job she has no interest in performing.

What are Carol's options? If she is like most of our clients, she will look into a supplemental disability insurance policy to fill the gap between what her company's disability insurance will pay and the total compensation her family and lifestyle depend on. The sample analysis I would run for someone like Carol is shown on the previous page, and compares the benefits paid by her employer-sponsored disability insurance plan, and a supplemental disability insurance policy.

Typically, most supplemental disability policies fill the gap up to eighty and ninety percent of your total income, including bonus pay. For Carol, her base salary as well as income from bonuses and restricted stock units or stock options would be covered.

Carol would also avoid a tax hit, since the benefits from a supplemental disability insurance policy (paid with her after-tax dollars) would be income-tax free upon disability. Also, the policy's definition of "disability" in a supplemental policy could be critically different than the employer provided plan. I often place supplemental policies with a definition that reads that she is "considered totally disabled if she is unable to perform the material and substantial duties of her regular occupation." Simply put, if she cannot perform the functions of her job, she would be considered disabled and would receive the benefits provided in the policy.

Additionally, if Carol is working with an advisor who has developed the specific knowledge of her employer's benefit plan and placed a lot of supplemental disability insurance with its employees (as our team has with Caterpillar Inc.), her advisor will likely be able to secure discounted "bulk" rates on her supplemental disability insurance coverage.

With a supplemental disability insurance plan in place to protect her income, Step 2 on Carol's Financial Security Checklist is complete. Her income is protected and she has insured one of the things she cannot afford to lose. We refer to this as a "cornerstone" in the financial house she is building. As she proceeds forward, having supplemental disability insurance in place with a financially stable insurance company that provides a strong contract definition will give her a solid foundation to build upon when moving to address her other financial goals.

CHAPTER SEVEN

STEP **3**

LIFE INSURANCE

NOW THAT CAROL HAS A COMPREHENSIVE financial plan and adequate disability insurance, Step 3 on her Financial Security Checklist continues to address the risk management component of her plan. Now Carol will need to evaluate the appropriate amount of life insurance both Walter, her husband, and she should carry to make sure their goals are met should one or both spouses pass away unexpectedly.

Life insurance is often the one type of insurance our clients like Carol have already started to address when our team first meets with them. At the same time, this preliminary planning often has gaps or inefficiencies. Carol's employer, for instance, provides group term-life insurance coverage at no cost. The coverage amount is a multiple of two times her base pay, not including bonus or any stock options. Therefore, because her base salary is $200,000, this equates to $400,000 of free group life insurance. In addition, she has the option to purchase up to an additional ten times ($2 million) her base pay in either term life insurance or guaranteed variable universal life insurance at her own personal expense. Carol can purchase up to $100,000 of term life insurance on her husband, Walter, and up to $10,000 of term life insurance on each of her two children, Ben and Ava. This means that if she chose to purchase the maximum for everyone in her family, she could have the free $400,000 plus an additional $2 million, for a total of $2.4 million of group life insurance coverage for herself, plus $100,000 for Walter and $10,000 for both Ben and Ava.

While these amounts might seem adequate, it is important that Carol discusses with her financial advisor what her priorities would be in the event she was to pass away unexpectedly. The peace of mind that comes from knowing her family would be okay in the event of an expected death is still elusive unless Carol is clear on what that $2.4 million of insurance will do.

The most common objectives for individuals like Carol who own life insurance include:

1. Paying outstanding debt,
2. Funding children's college education,
3. Funding final expenses, such as a funeral, attorney's fees, and probate (if applicable),
4. Replacing income to sustain the family's lifestyle, and
5. Leaving a planned legacy.

Note that this is a general list, and each client our team works with has his or her own specific objectives.

As a part of Step 1 (creating a comprehensive plan), a good advisor will have taken the time to understand Carol's personal situation and ensure that the amount of coverage she is carrying is adequate to meet her objectives. Some financial planning textbooks would suggest a rule of thumb that Carol should carry between eight to twelve times her income in life insurance ($1.6 million to $2.4 million), but no textbook guideline can replace a trusted advisor helping her evaluate and ensure that her coverage matches her individual goals.

This same process should be applied to Walter, Ben, and Ava in determining an adequate amount of coverage in the event they die unexpectedly. Rarely is the additional coverage available to purchase through Carol's employer adequate, and while difficult to think about such scenarios, the process is important.

Once the appropriate amount of coverage is calculated, Carol needs to compare the cost structure for the optional life insurance offered through her employer. While the rates provided are often competitive at younger ages, she will find that they increase exponentially every five years. Therefore, it is often more efficient from a cost perspective to own her life insurance outside of her employer, which is true for many of our Caterpillar Inc. clients. On many occasions, we have found that someone like Carol could save tens of thousands of dollars in life insurance premiums over a lifetime by owning that coverage through an individual life insurance policy outside of the employer.

Another thought for Carol to consider is the likelihood she will be working for her current employer her entire career. She currently has every intention to continue with the company long-term, but she also knows nothing is guaranteed. She has seen several peers lose their jobs in past economic downturns, so she recognizes the value of having important benefits like life insurance owned outside of her company.

Lastly, there is certainly no guarantee that her employer will maintain the current level of benefits and cost structure going forward. Carol has more peace of mind since she owns a portion of her life insurance coverage individually, independent of her company and possible changes in its benefits.

Regardless of how much coverage Carol chooses, and no matter the insurance company or type (Term, Permanent, or Universal), one thing is certain: Step 3 in Carol's financial plan should include an in-depth conversation with her financial advisor to ensure her life insurance planning is in alignment with her personal goals.

CHAPTER EIGHT

STEP  4

ESTATE PLANNING

AS CAROL PUTS THE FINISHING TOUCHES on her risk management planning, Step 4 is to create appropriate and up-to-date estate plans, such as wills and trusts.

Like disability and life insurance, this is an area most individuals clearly recognize as important, but often fail to find the time to implement. While our team, like most financial planning teams, does not give legal advice, we do believe estate planning is a critical piece to Carol's financial plan.

I have heard it said that "drama is in the details" when an estate is being settled. Carol's last, best gift to her family is planning inheritance details ahead of time so that her family can gather together to heal rather than argue over the details of the estate plan.

NEED FOR A WILL

Let's start with the importance of a basic will. Carol, like most of our clients, is likely unaware of all the consequences of not having this in place. In addition to specifying how assets are distributed, arguably the most important aspect of a will may be to designate guardianship of her minor children (which is categorized as any child under the age of eighteen or twenty-one, depending on the state in which you live).

Simply put, who will raise Ben and Ava if both Carol and Walter were to pass away? Without a will in place to provide direction in this area, the local court system or judge will make that decision. This means that someone who likely knows nothing about Carol's family will determine which of her family will raise her children.

While that may not sound like a problem to some people, this is very disturbing to Carol. When thinking about her close family, she recognizes some family members whom she sees as great parents and others whom she simply cannot see in that role for Ben and Ava. There may even be a few she thinks have no business parenting! (Can you relate?)

In fact, she and Walter would prefer that one of their close friends, who shares their values, be Ben and Ava's guardians rather than a family member. Without a will in place, the local court system or judge will ultimately have the final say, and the courts might choose family over friends. The thought of the court system having the final decision is quite scary to Carol and Walter, and most parents share this worry.

NEED FOR A TRUST

In addition to a will, our clients like Carol will often have an attorney establish a trust to protect assets in the event both spouses pass away, and the children are not yet old enough to handle the responsibility of managing those resources. For example, assuming Carol owns $2.4 million of life insurance and Walter owns another $1 million, there would be a total of $3.4 million of life insurance proceeds in the event they both pass away together.

The idea of Ben and Ava getting $3.4 million when turning 18 or 21, depending on the state in which they live, with no strings attached, is quite scary for any parent. Will they use the money to go to college? Spend the weekend in Vegas? This is probably not a question a teenager should be deciding.

While Carol hopes Ben and Ava would be responsible with the money, she remembers some of the decisions she made at that age and fears her children making some of those same mistakes.

All this worry is solved with the establishment of a trust. In short, the trust would become the contingent (secondary) beneficiary of all assets (including life insurance policies), and the trust would be managed by a trustee who, with the guidance of trust documents, would determine how trust funds would be disseminated.

If either Carol or Walter dies, the surviving spouse would become the primary beneficiary and receive all assets. The money would be directed to the trust and the contingent beneficiary only if both spouses both die together, for example by car crash or other tragic accident.

Without a trust, Carol's beneficiary designations on life insurance policies become more risky. If Carol does not have a trust in place for her minor children, she would likely list her parents as the contingent (secondary) beneficiaries on the insurance policy in the event she and Walter both die at the same time. While Carol has one hundred percent confidence in her parents' ability to handle the life insurance proceeds, and to direct the funds to Ava and Ben at the appropriate age, what happens if her parents are sued over a their own car accident? The life insurance funds intended for Ben and Ava could be lost in a lawsuit. What if her parents fall on hard times due to an economic downturn, and they are forced to use the funds in bankruptcy court? The insurance proceeds would be listed in their names as unprotected assets, and they could be at risk.

All the life insurance planning could be for nothing if Carol and Walter do not establish a trust and list it is as the contingent (secondary) beneficiary on their policies.

Certainly, these examples are not all inclusive, and there are many other reasons for Carol to have her estate planning in place. But these examples should be enough to motivate her to reach out to an attorney and start the process of creating an estate plan. Our team's advice for Carol is to work with an attorney who spends a good majority, if not all of his or her time, working in the field of estate planning. To use a medical analogy, she would not want to get advice from her dermatologist in the event she needed heart surgery. Sure, the dermatologist is a physician, but he or she is not a specialist in heart surgery.

Along the same lines, she would not want to assume that a divorce, real estate, or general practice attorney is the best choice to prepare her estate plans.

At this stage of her planning, Carol is well on her way as she creates her roadmap to financial security. She has worked with a financial advisor to complete a comprehensive financial plan, her income is protected with adequate disability insurance, and she has protected her family in the event of an unexpected death with the right amount of life insurance.

And now she has the peace of mind that comes with completing Step 4 in her financial checklist: establishing an estate plan that includes wills and trusts.

CHAPTER NINE

STEP 5

EMERGENCY FUND

AS CAROL FURTHER DEVELOPS HER ROADMAP, Step 5 will be to plan for unexpected detours. She must establish an adequate emergency fund. While different sources will provide slightly different answers, a good general guideline will be to have three to six months of living expenses set aside. If her household monthly expenses—including mortgage, groceries, and the like—total $5,000 per month, she would target $15,000 to $30,000 to set aside for her emergency fund. This prevents Carol from being forced to use credit cards and other expensive options when unexpected setbacks happen.

It is important to be clear on what qualifies as a true emergency fund. Many people use their savings account to accomplish different things, like setting aside funds to pay for property taxes, future vacations, and emergencies. We think it is wise to distinguish between what we call a true "savings account," which is used for emergencies, and a "deferred spending account," which would be used for future planned expenses like those property taxes and a vacation.

The savings account does not need to be anything fancy. Carol can establish this at no cost through her local bank. She just needs to put the money somewhere that can be easily accessed in the event a real emergency arises. No one wants to wait a week for funds to transfer, and no one wants to see their emergency fund dissipate due to market fluctuations!

This true savings account is the account in which to hold that three to six months of living expenses. And then you discipline yourself not to use it, except in case of emergency.

Often people have money in an account they call their "savings account," but they use the money for planned expenses. For planned expenses, they should consider a savings account separate from their emergency fund, and think of it as their "deferred spending account." A deferred spending account is not really for savings and it is definitely not a dedicated emergency fund.

For instance, if Carol plans on using the money in her savings account for birthday presents for her two children, these are planned expenses and could be paid for using her deferred spending account. This leaves the three- to six-months' worth of living expenses safely tucked away in her emergency fund savings account available for true emergencies. When the roof unexpectedly needs to be replaced, the car suddenly dies, or illness or injury brings a slew of expenses, her financial plans are not derailed and she can quickly access needed funds without worrying about giving up the vacation or paying the tax bill.

Sound reasonable? The three to six months of expenses she should have set aside for potential emergencies should never be earmarked for other purchases. Often the easiest way of accomplishing this is simply having two separate accounts. Thinking of them distinctly as a savings account and a deferred spending account helps Carol stay on course with budgeting and gives the peace of mind that a true emergency fund gives. This is not overly complicated, but it is important for the sake of clarity: The three to six months of living expenses are earmarked for unexpected emergencies, setbacks, and expenses, not vacations, birthday presents, and property taxes.

With an emergency fund, Step 5 of her Financial Security Checklist is complete.

CHAPTER TEN

STEP 6

DEBT REDUCTION

ONCE STEP 1 THROUGH STEP 5 are complete, Carol can begin to get traction. In Step 6 of her Financial Security Checklist, Carol will want to begin aggressively addressing her debt. This includes credit cards, car loans, and student loans.

Emotionally, this was a hard one for Carol to swallow because, as I mentioned, she is conservative, and therefore hates the idea of debt. It was hard for her to prioritize building the emergency fund over making debt payments.

Many of our clients can certainly relate. While we are not proponents of our clients carrying unnecessary debt, we do believe that Carol made the right choice in prioritizing her emergency fund over making extra payments on her debt. Other nationally respected financial resources[6,7], support this notion as well, but some suggest starting with $1,000 in the emergency fund instead of the full three to

---

6   E. F. c. Carter, "Forbes.com," 6 March 2014. [Online]. Available: https://www.forbes.com/sites/financialfinesse/2014/03/06/should-you-increase-savings-first-or-pay-down-debt/#54c152284914. [Accessed 12 April 2017].

7   K. q. S. O. i. Palmer, "US News," 3 April 2009. [Online]. Available: http://money.usnews.com/money/personal-finance/articles/2009/04/03/suze-orman-and-the-new-rules-of-credit-card-debt. [Accessed 12 April 2017].

six months of expenses. Taking this approach would allow Carol to more quickly pay down higher-interest debt instead of waiting to pay down debt while building the three-to-six-month emergency fund.

Either way, having some level of emergency fund should take priority over making extra payments on debt. If Carol instead chooses to pay extra on her home mortgage before developing an adequate emergency fund, she leaves her family exposed in the event an emergency arises.

Where would she go to get the money for the new roof without the emergency fund? I doubt that the mortgage company is going to be very cooperative if Carol asks them to return the extra payments. Assuming she doesn't have family to bail her out, she would be looking at less attractive and more costly options like borrowing from her credit cards or taking a loan from her 401(k).

Bottom line, Step 6 of debt reduction comes after Step 5 of establishing an emergency fund for a good reason.

Fortunately for Carol, outside of her mortgage, she does not carry much additional debt.

That is not always the case, though, and our clients often ask how to prioritize their debt-reduction plans and save and invest for the future. Certainly, if you have unsecured debt with excessively high interest rates, like credit cards, you will want to pay them off as quickly as possible.

If your debt is at a lower interest rate, many financial advisors might argue to pay the minimums and invest the extra you would have paid. Mathematically, the numbers often show that this is the wise financial decision in the long run. That said, our perspective is that the extent to which our clients aggressively tackle their debt is a personal choice. While it could make financial sense to make minimum payments and invest everything else into investments that should earn more over the long run, typically the earnings are not guaranteed and many people cannot put a price tag or calculate an interest rate on the peace of mind that comes from being debt-free.

A good financial advisor is going to seek to truly understand your feelings on debt and help you develop a plan that is aligned with your goals. Step 6 states: pay off your credit cards, or any unsecured high interest debt, as quickly as possible, and develop a plan for the rest.

CHAPTER ELEVEN

STEP 7

RETIREMENT PLANNING

ASSUMING CAROL HAS SUCCESSFULLY EXECUTED the risk management portion of her financial plan, she can feel very confident that she is protected in the event of an unexpected event. Her risks are covered. Nick Murray, author and financial planning guru, would say Carol has "insured against what can go wrong in order to acquire the luxury of investing for what can go right."[8]

Moving onto the wealth accumulation portion of her financial plan, Carol's first question will likely be, "How much should I be saving?"

While there are many rules of thumb, online calculators, and guidelines, the specific answer to this question comes back to Step 1 in the Financial Security Checklist. Carol should look at the comprehensive financial plan she created, since the plan will drive what needs to be implemented. The plan will tell her how much she needs to be saving.

Every plan is unique because every client's story is unique. Therefore, rules of thumb may not be enough.

---

8   N. Murray, *Game of Numbers*.

That said, it is important to establish realistic expectations. The expectation we set with our clients is that they will need to be saving at least fifteen percent of their gross income, with a goal of getting to twenty percent. The old notion that saving ten percent of your income will get you to your goals is no longer feasible in light of companies doing away with their pension plans, and with Social Security becoming less and less reliable.

For Carol, Step 8 will be setting a goal to save twenty percent of her income long term.

WHERE TO START?

The second question Carol will ask is, "Where do I start?"

Should she begin planning for Ben and Ava's college? She and Walter consider it a priority and want to cover one hundred percent of the cost of their children's' education. Should she start addressing their goal of becoming financially independent and able to retire by age sixty?

> ## IF YOU ARE CONFUSED ABOUT WHERE TO START, CONTACT ME AT JOSHWAITE@UPANDDOWNTHEMOUNTAIN.COM

For many clients like Carol, these are not easy questions to answer for emotional reasons. Because Carol is like most of the clients we work with, she loves Ben and Ava dearly, has sacrificed in the past, and would sacrifice in the future to provide for them. Therefore, her inclination is to establish a college savings plan for their future college costs prior to focusing on retirement goals.

Carol could be making a mistake if she allows her emotions to drive her decision-making. The truth is this is a very logical decision.

Let me explain.

RETIREMENT V. EDUCATION

With the assistance of her financial advisor team, Carol realizes that while there is no denying her love for Ben and Ava and her subsequent desire to provide for them in the future, she must focus on her retirement goals first, even if doing so means not having enough money saved to fully fund their college education. The reason is simple. When Ben and Ava reach college age, they will likely have several options to cover the costs including student loans, grants, and scholarships. Simply put, there are ways to pay for college if someone is motivated to find them.

Alternatively, should Carol and Walter choose to save for Ben and Ava's college first, they risk arriving at their desired retirement age without enough funds to adequately support themselves financially. Currently, there are no government loans to fund retirement.

Emotionally the choice might be tough, but logically it is an easy one: Save for retirement first, education second. Therefore, Carol will want to prioritize retirement before they put resources towards Ben and Ava's future college education.

Now that Carol knows to start with her retirement planning before Ben and Ava's college, she will need to think through her options for retirement. She starts with what is offered through her employer, and it does not take long before she is overwhelmed.

She has a dizzying array of options: traditional pension, pension equity plan, 401(k), Roth 401(k), company match, restricted stock units, stock appreciation rights, and the list goes on. Fortunately for Carol, her financial advisor team has many years of experience and very specialized knowledge in understanding and maximizing the nuances of her employer's retirement benefits. Considering her employer retirement benefits will likely be the largest component of her retirement planning, having a thorough understanding of the available choices and how they work is critical. The truth is, many advisors will suggest to clients that they are knowledgeable of her benefits, but they often do not fully understand every nuance of the different plans. Since Carol's team does, let's dive in!

401(K) PLAN

The 401(k) plan will be Carol's most significant component of her retirement plan. Therefore, she needs to understand how to maximize it.

Let's start with the question, "How much should I contribute?"

This will ultimately tie back to her specific goals outlined in her comprehensive financial plan. But the first and most important point for Carol to remember is simple: Always take full advantage of the company match.

For Carol's employer, the match is dollar-for-dollar on the first six percent she contributes of both her base pay (salary) and bonus. This point is very important: Many of Carol's peers think the match is for base pay only, so they contribute six percent of just their base pay. This means they are missing out on some of the employer's potential match.

If Carol contributes both six percent of her base pay and six percent of her bonus/incentive earnings, the company makes a match that is the equivalent of Carol receiving a six percent bonus.

For Carol, it is a no-brainer to at least contribute six percent to her 401(k). As a part of the financial planning process Carol's financial advisor team will take her through, she will also be able to identify any additional amount she should be contributing to her 401(k) plan. After that, they should determine how much she should be saving for retirement outside of her 401(k) to reach her goals for financial independence.

TRADITIONAL V. ROTH 401(K)

In addition to determining the appropriate amount to contribute, Carol's employer offers both a Traditional 401(k) plan and a Roth 401(k). She can either contribute to the Traditional, the Roth, or a combination of both.

The primary distinction between a Traditional 401(k) and a Roth 401(k) is the tax treatment, both at the time she makes a contribution and at retirement when she takes a distribution.

With the Traditional 401(k), all of Carol's contributions are made on a pre-tax basis. This means that when she contributes $10,000 into the plan, her taxable income will reduce by $10,000. So if her salary plus incentive pay totals $250,000, she will only be taxed on $240,000 for that specific year. She has an upfront tax savings with the Traditional 401(k), but the taxes are deferred and will need to be paid when she retires and is ready to use the funds.

In addition, while the money is invested inside the plan, it grows on a tax-deferred basis. Simply put, she pays no tax on the interest each year. While this sounds attractive, Carol must remember that she has not permanently avoided the tax. She instead has simply kicked the can down the road. When she retires and begins taking money out, she will pay ordinary income tax on her contribution (the $10,000), the company match, and all her gains and interest earned over the years.

On the other hand, if she makes the same $10,000 contribution to the Roth 401(k), this contribution will be made on an after-tax basis. This means that she receives no tax deduction or tax savings today. Assuming she earns $250,000 of income, she will be taxed on $250,000 of income.

So, what is the benefit to Carol with the Roth? The tax

savings come at the time she is ready to retire and use the funds. In contrast to the Traditional 401(k), where she paid income tax at the time of distribution, with a Roth, she will pay no tax on the funds when she pulls money out in retirement. She will not have to pay tax on her original contribution amounts ($10,000, in the example here), nor on the gains earned.

So the difference is: When do you want to pay tax?

"Never" is an understandable, but invalid, answer! With Traditional 401(k)s, you pay the tax when you retire and access the funds. With Roth 401(k)s, your contributions are made with money that was already taxed as income.

COMMON MISCONCEPTIONS

One point of confusion for Carol (and many of our clients) is that she has heard about an income limit for Roth 401(k) plans. Someone told her, or she read somewhere, that she makes too much money to contribute to a Roth.

This limitation refers to the IRS income limitations placed on Roth IRAs (Individual Retirement Accounts). Fortunately for Carol, these income limits do not apply to Roth 401(k) plans. Therefore, she (and you) can participate regardless of income.

Another important note is this: Regardless of whether Carol contributes to the Traditional 401(k) or the Roth 401(k), her employer still makes the matching contributions (for example, the six percent match) into the Traditional 401(k). Carol would not forfeit her match by using the Roth 401(k).

LEVERAGING BOTH PLANS

So, which is better? It will depend on the specifics of Carol's financial situation, along with both her current and future tax rates. If she knew that her tax bracket at retirement would be higher than it is today, the Roth 401(k) could make more sense since she will pay no income tax when she takes distributions. If she knew that her tax bracket at retirement would be lower than it is today, the Traditional 401(k) might make more sense, because she would have avoided tax now at the higher rate, and then be pulling money out in retirement at a lower rate.

The problem is, no one knows with certainty what tax brackets or rates will be twenty or thirty years into the future. As a general rule, then, Carol might consider leveraging both plans. In doing so, she will have flexibility when the time comes to begin taking distributions. She can make strategic choices: If tax brackets are high one year, she could pull more from her Roth 401(k). If tax brackets are low another year, she can pull more from her Traditional 401(k).

During her high-earning years, when she is contributing to her 401(k) plans, whether Roth or Traditional, Carol must make specific investment elections on how she will want her money invested within the 401(k)s. Is she aggressive (willing to take more risk) or conservative (wanting to be more safe)? Is she in stocks or bonds? Mutual funds or company stock? Does she manage the investments herself, or does she take the have-the-company-do-it-for-you approach? Since every individual investor's goals, experience, and risk tolerance is unique, Carol will want to work with her financial planning team to make sure the allocation of investments in her 401(k) plans matches her goals for retirement.

Step 8 on Carol's Financial Security Checklist will be for her to diversify her retirement assets from a tax perspective, providing flexibility, options, and the ability to be more strategic when it is time to access funds. Her financial planning team should also help her determine her risk profile and make sure investments within her 401(k)s align with her goals.

DEFERRED COMPENSATION PLAN

Carol's company, like many Fortune 500 companies,

offers a deferred compensation plan[9] for some executives above a certain salary level. In my years of experience with clients at Caterpillar Inc., I have often seen executives who were losing out on "free" money due to common misconceptions about this benefit and how it relates to retirement funding.

Basically, a deferred compensation plan allows you to contribute more money above and beyond the 401(k) contribution limits into a pre-tax retirement plan. Inside that pre-tax retirement plan, you are able to invest and allocate your money in a similar fashion to what you are doing inside the current 401(k) plans.

What I have observed is many individuals do not take advantage of this plan simply due to a lack of understanding. They assume there is no benefit to them because they are already maxing out the IRS limits on what they can contribute to a 401(k). While that may be the case for some individuals, for others, it is not. And the purpose of a deferred compensation plan in its design was actually to give individuals whose total compensation (salary plus bonus) goes over a set IRS threshold an opportunity to receive matching contributions on income earned over that amount.

Another way to say this is: If their income is over that IRS limit and they do **not** use the supplemental deferred compensation plan, they may be missing out on a portion of the company match. They may be missing out on money that their employer is offering them simply by not electing to participate.

There are a lot of details and complexities related to a deferred compensation plan that you should certainly

---

9 **Disclosures re: Deferred Compensation Plan:** It should be noted that a Deferred Compensation Plan (DCP) does not have the same creditor protections as a qualified plan, like a 401(k). Generally, the funds put in the DCP may not be accelerated once an initial deferral time frame is set; however, payments may be delayed subject to certain tax rules. No rollovers to an IRA are permitted from the DCP plan. Consult your attorney and your tax advisor if you have further questions about the legal and tax structure of the DCP.

talk through with your financial advisor. We walk our clients through the program, simplify the details, and make it understandable. We then have an annual review process to ensure this opportunity is not missed.

Make sure your financial planning team has a detailed understanding of the complexities of a deferred compensation plan, as well as the software and financial planning expertise to analyze the best options to recommend to you.

PENSION

In addition to Carol's different 401(k) plan options and deferred compensation plan options, she also is fortunate to still have an employer-sponsored defined benefit pension plan. These plans are provided by an employer in which the contributions are not made by Carol but are instead fully funded by the employer. The money is invested by the employer, and then paid out to Carol in the form of a monthly pension benefit when she retires. While many employers of all sizes have moved away from providing these plans, Carol is one of the fortunate ones to still have this benefit.

Since the employer funds the plan, Carol does not have a choice on how much to contribute or how to invest. Simply put, while she is working, there are no decisions that need to be made. In anticipation of her retirement, her company will present her with a variety of options about how and when to receive pension payments.

The pension election is a one-time, irrevocable decision. Once the decision is made, Carol cannot go back and change it. She and Walter need to make this decision carefully, weighing the pros and cons of her various options with an experienced financial advisor.

Originally, Carol thought her pension payment decisions should be put off until the eve of retirement. She loves her job and, at age fifty, she doesn't see herself retiring soon. As she progresses through her financial planning checklist, though, she soon realizes she is at an ideal spot to think through pension decisions.

She and Walter will have several different pension payout options:

- Single-life annuity.

    Under this option, Carol and Walter would receive $10,000[10] per month until Carol's death. Upon Carol's death, payments would stop and Walter would receive nothing.

    At first, Carol is attracted to the single-life payout because its monthly payout is the highest that the plan offers. But she understands that if she dies before Walter, the payments stop altogether, and he gets nothing.

- Joint and survivor annuity.

    With this payout option, the pension will pay until the end of Carol's lifetime, and then will continue to pay Walter for his lifetime. Because the payments are more likely to continue for a longer period of time, Carol will receive less money each month during her lifetime than with a single life payout.

    Carol and Walter have several choices here: With a "joint and survivor 100% option," they will receive a monthly payment of $8,000. If Carol predeceases Walter, Walter still receives the $8,000 pension.

    With a "joint and survivor 75% option," the payout climbs to $9,000 per month while Carol is alive, but will drop to $6,750 per month after her death. In addition, Carol's company offers a few more variations of these two.

---

10    $10,000 is used as an example only, actual amount may vary depending on the plan.

Should Carol elect single life annuity and buy life insurance on herself?

As Carol and Walter think through their options, they decide they are more comfortable with the annuity option. They like the higher monthly payments and hope to replace the income that Walter will not be receiving after his death with proceeds of a life insurance policy Carol owns on herself. Here's how that analysis might go:

- If Carol and Walter had opted for the "joint and survivor 100% annuity," they would have received monthly payments of $8,000. Assuming a forty percent income tax rate, this leaves $4,800 per month after tax.

- To determine the amount of death benefit from a life insurance policy that will be needed to produce a similar monthly payout, Carol and her financial advisor consult a Minimum Payment Rate Table and crunch the numbers. Together, they determine that Carol's death benefit need is $1.5 million, which will allow Walter to receive a monthly payout close to the $4,800 a month pension that the "joint and survivor 100% annuity" would have paid.

Considerations regarding life insurance

1. Buying a life policy *upon* retirement works in some situations, but depends on the health rating Carol would qualify for. It is important to be cautious when thinking Carol can use the "excess" payout—the difference between the payouts for single and joint life annuities—to purchase a life insurance policy at or around retirement. Generally, life insurance premiums rise as people age. This is where a knowledgeable financial planning team should crunch the numbers and help you determine if it makes sense for you.

2. For many people, it works best if the policy is bought well *before* retirement. If Carol has a pre-existing policy, it could be earmarked to replace the income that Walter would forego if she chooses a single-life annuity and predeceases him. For example, assume Carol owns a life insurance policy with a death benefit of $1.5 million that she purchased when she was younger. Now she could elect the larger single-life annuity payout knowing that if she dies before Walter, he can use the tax-free death benefit from the life insurance. And if Walter dies first, Carol still receives the larger single-life pension payments and can use the life insurance to provide a legacy for their children.

For clients who are lucky enough to still participate in pension plans, the decision of which payout to choose is something that should be planned in advance. One way to preserve the most options is to buy the appropriate amount of life insurance well before retirement age.

The earlier this possibility is discussed by financial advisors and clients, the more likely the numbers will work.[11,12]

Since the pension payout decisions are irrevocable and can only be made at the point of retirement, it is critical to work with a financial planning team that can help with this decision. Once you choose your path down this part of the mountain, there is no turning back. If Carol decides on a single annuity option, her financial advisor should have the necessary tools and knowledge to calculate exactly how much life insurance it would take to replace the amount of

---

11   Northwestern Mutual Life Insurance Company, Advanced Planning Library, Factors Affecting the Decision of Which Pension Payout to Take, 2013.

12   **Disclosures regarding pensions:** This publication is not intended as legal or tax advice. It must not be used as a basis for legal or tax advice, and is not intended to be used and cannot be used to avoid any penalties that may be imposed on a taxpayers. Taxpayers should seek advice regarding their particular circumstances from an independent tax advisor.

pension payout lost.

What appeared on the surface to be a pretty easy decision was actually much more complicated than Carol originally thought. With proper guidance, she will not only get the maximum benefit from her pension, but she may also get a life insurance policy that provides added security for herself and her family.

EQUITY COMPENSATION

The final element of compensation that can have a significant effect on Carol's retirement planning is the different forms of equity compensation she receives. Equity compensation from a Fortune 500 company often comes in different forms, but for Carol it is in Restricted Stock Units (RSUs), Stock Appreciation Rights (SARs), and Non-Qualified stock options (NQs). All three forms are ultimately affected by the performance of her company stock, but how they operate, and how they are treated from a tax perspective, vary greatly.

RESTRICTED STOCK UNITS

Let's begin with Restricted Stock Units (RSUs). RSUs are granted to Carol each year in the spring. What she receives is a set number of shares of company stock that are "restricted," meaning that Carol may not sell the shares until they "vest." This gives Carol an incentive to stick with the company to see those shares vest, and also aligns her interests with shareholders who are hoping for employees who do their best to help the company hit its goals and targets.

VESTING TIME TABLE

Vesting simply means that over time, the restriction is lifted and Carol may then sell the shares. Vesting schedules have varied over the years. In 2017, the vesting schedule for Carol's employer was: one-third, one-third, one-third.

Let me explain.

For the first year following the grant of the stock, Carol

was restricted from doing anything with her RSUs—they all remain restricted. At the one-year anniversary, one-third of her shares are vested, meaning one-third of her shares are now hers to use as she chooses. In Year Two, the second one-third of shares vest, and in Year Three, the final one-third vest. Every year a new block of 300 restricted shares is granted and will vest on the same schedule of one-third each year. This table shows a visual example with grants of 100 shares as an example.

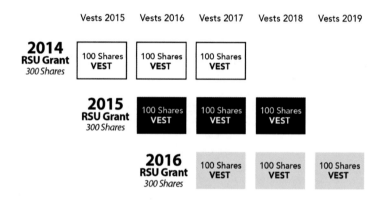

TAX CONSIDERATIONS

Upon vesting, the fair market value of those shares is reported as income to Carol. Her company will calculate the amount of wages to report and will withhold the appropriate amount of federal, state, and FICA taxes on those wages, and report it all on her W-2 for the current year.

With many companies, the withholding tax is taken in the form of reduced shares issued to Carol. Carol will then receive a deposit in her account representing the net number of shares of stock that are now free and clear for her to do with as she wishes.

Does all of this sound simple, clear, and easy to understand? If you are anything like Carol and Walter, and the many other clients I have discussed this with over the years, my guess is that "clear as mud" may be your answer.

Let's look at a quick example for clarity.

Assume Carol was granted 300 shares in March of 2014. According to the vesting schedule, in March of 2015, 100 shares will vest. If the stock price at that time is $75 per share, Carol will have $7,500 (100 x $75) of wages reported on her W-2. Her employer will determine the amount of tax (federal, state, and FICA) to withhold on the wages.

Let's assume that the total withholding taxes are $2,550. Her company will then calculate how many shares are needed to fulfill that tax-withholding requirement. In Carol's case, 34 shares would be needed ($2,550 / $75 = 34). Carol will now receive 66 shares of stock (100 − 34) in her account (with a cost basis of $75 per share) that she may do with whatever she likes.

It's important to note that the employer tax withholding on special forms of compensation such as this is often less than needed to fully cover the taxes that will be incurred when filing one's tax return. Typically employers withhold only 25 percent federal tax when many people like Carol are in much higher effective federal tax brackets. As a result, Carol will be responsible for any additional taxes that may be required when her tax return is filed the following year.

The following year, March 2016, Carol will have the same process take place for the next third of her RSUs. And finally, in March of 2017, the final third will vest and become available for Carol to access.

Now may be a good point to pause and comment on a few observations we have made with nearly all clients we have worked with who receive RSU grants like Carol:

1. They are surprised at tax time, and usually not in a good way.
2. They are confused on where the stock they receive is deposited.
3. If they can find where the shares were deposited,

they do not understand what choices they now have with those shares.

4. If they actually find the shares and understand they can now sell them, they have no idea what the cost basis is in the shares and how selling them effects their tax return.

An advisor who can confidently provide insight and explanations to all aspects of RSUs, and help clear up confusion around this form of compensation, will allow Carol to sleep much better at night.

In the context of Carol's broader financial plan, her advisor can now show her how she may begin thinking of her RSUs as a deferred bonus plan she will receive every year, as long as she remains employed at her company. What she does with the stock once it vests will be determined by the goals of her overall financial plan. She may continue to hold the stock until a later date with hopes that the price will go up, and she will benefit from the appreciation. She may alternatively sell the shares immediately and use the proceeds to fund other goals within her financial plan.

As long as she has completed Step 1 with that comprehensive financial plan in place, it should be easy for her to determine how to best leverage her Restricted Stock Units to meet her goal of financial security.

STOCK APPRECIATION RIGHTS AND NON-QUALIFIED STOCK OPTIONS

Let's now turn to Stock Appreciation Rights (SARs) and Non-Qualified stock options (NQs). Carol has received both forms of compensation in the past. Subtle differences exist between a SAR and an NQ, but I will not focus on those differences in this book. Instead, I will refer to them both simply as "stock options."

Stock options are very different from RSUs both in how they function and how they are treated from a tax standpoint. They are, after all, stock options, not shares of stock. In the most basic of terms, they give Carol the choice of buying a fixed number of shares of stock shares at a fixed price over a stated period of years.

The fixed price is called the strike price. The stated number of years is the maturity date. The options granted to Carol have a maturity of ten years. She will have ten years to determine at what point in time she wishes to exercise her option, or she may choose to not exercise her option at all. The term "exercise" simply means Carol chooses to exercise her right to purchase the stock at the fixed price. After the maturity date, the option expires and Carol can no longer exercise it.

The strike price for the option is the prevailing price of stock on the date of grant—which is the same grant date each year as the RSUs. As with RSUs, Carol's options also have a one-third, one-third, and one-third vesting period. Once vested, Carol may exercise the option. Prior to vesting, exercises are not allowed.

Unlike RSUs, upon vesting, no income is reported on Carol's W-2. The tax reporting for stock options will not happen until Carol exercises the option.

So to recap, each March, Carol receives a grant—a right to purchase stock at the current stock price—and that strike price is fixed for a ten-year period until it is at maturity. It's like locking in a stock price for ten years, so if the company does well and the stock goes up, Carol still gets to buy it for less than the current market price.

But what if her company's stock doesn't increase in price? What does Carol do with her option? Nothing?

Bingo! Correct!

As you can see, Carol only receives a benefit from options if the price of stock increases and she exercises her option. As stated, this is very different from RSUs which always have a value (assuming the company's stock will al-

JOSHUA T. WAITE

ways have value) In simple terms, RSUs are a gift of stock, whereas NQs and SARs are options to purchase stock at potentially below-market price.

Let's look at a specific example:

Assume Carol was granted 3,000 options (NQ stock options) in March of 2014 at a strike price of $100. In March of 2015, 1,000 of the NQ stock options will vest. In contrast to her RSUs, no tax is due on those stock options because she only has the option to buy the shares. Until she actually chooses to exercise that option, there are no tax implications.

If she sees that her company's stock price is lower than her strike price, she can just ignore her option. Again there are no tax implications. In March of 2016, another 1,000 shares will vest. And lastly, in March of 2017, the final 1,000 shares will vest. Again, vesting simply means she now has access to do what she wants with them and can exercise the option to sell them at any point between the vesting date and the maturity date of March 2024 when the option expires.

Let us further assume that it is now March of 2022 and her company stock is trading at $125 per share. Carol decides that now is a good time to exercise her 3,000 NQ stock options that have vested. There are different methods Carol can use to exercise the option. We will look at two examples, one called a "swap sale," and the other called a "swap and hold."

EXERCISING OPTIONS USING SWAP SALE

The economic benefit Carol receives from the exercise can be determined by taking the current stock price ($125) minus the option strike price ($100) multiplied by the number of options exercised (3,000). Therefore, the economic benefit is $75,000. This is the amount her employer will report on Carol's W-2 as wages. The company will also withhold taxes on the exercise. Assume total tax withholding required is $27,250. As such, Carol will receive a net check for $47,750 ($75,000 - $27,250). The "swap sale" method of exercising an option results in cash to Carol.

EXERCISING OPTIONS USING SWAP AND HOLD

If Carol had instead chosen to exercise her option using a "swap and hold" exercise, she will end up with shares of stock in hand, instead of cash.

Let us illustrate using the same example above.

Carol's economic benefit is still the same $75,000. The tax-withholding requirement is also the same at $27,250. As with RSUs, the company will satisfy the tax withholding by reducing the number of shares provided to Carol. For this exercise, 218 shares would be needed ($27,250 / $125= 218).

So how many shares of stock will Carol receive?

She will receive 382 shares.

Here's why: Her economic benefit is $75,000. That equates to 600 shares ($75,000 / $125). The company needs to withhold 218 shares for taxes as determined previously. So the net number of shares Carol receives is 382 (600-218).

What is her cost basis in the stock? It's $125, the current market value.

Similar to RSUs, Carol may now choose what she wishes to do with these shares. She could sell them right away for $125 each and have no capital gain or loss on the sale. Alternatively, she could hold the shares and sell at a later date. Any capital gain or loss on the sale would be determined by the price of stock on the date of sale, less her cost basis per share of $125.

CONSIDERATIONS UPON RETIREMENT

Now that Carol understands the mechanics of her options, she will certainly want to maximize the value of this element of her total compensation package.

When should she exercise? What price is considered a good price? How should she plan for the tax consequences?

All are great questions her financial planning team should be able to answer.

WHEN TO EXERCISE OPTIONS

In our work with clients at Caterpillar, we have developed a formula to provide clients with a reasonable range one should expect to be able to exercise options. We certainly cannot predict what stock price will do. But we can confidently give our clients a reasonable range based upon historical factual data that they can then use as guardrails to help determine at what point in time to sell. We also help our clients fully understand the tax implications of exercising options in a given year, which prevents surprises when tax time comes around.

MATURITY DATE

Once Carol reaches retirement, she has additional considerations to be aware of regarding her equity grants. The first is that the Maturity Date of the options will be adjusted. At her company, like many others, she will not be given the full ten years to exercise her options after retiring. Instead, she will be given the lesser of the remaining years on that particular option, or five years.

So if Carol retires in 2017, her 2014 option will expire in March of 2022 (five years from the date of retirement, not the original Maturity Date of March 2024). This is important to remember as Carol is planning out her early retirement years. After all, she will likely have higher income her first five years after retirement due to options that will need to be exercised. Additionally, any RSUs that Carol has remaining will automatically vest six months following her retirement. Therefore, she could have three years of RSUs all vesting in the year of her retirement.

This is great, right?

It is true that she will receive several shares of stock to help fund her retirement, but think about the tax consequences. This creates a lot of wage income to be reported on her W-2.

How much tax will she owe? Are there ways to avoid some of that tax, or at least minimize the effect? Both of these are great questions for Carol to ask her financial planning team.

TARGET OWNERSHIP REQUIREMENTS

Lastly, it is important for Carol to pay close attention to how many total shares of company stock she owns. Her company, like many others, has had a required number of shares she needs to maintain to continue receiving future grants, be it RSUs or NQ/SAR stock options. This is referred to as target ownership requirements. Though Carol's employer has recently eliminated this requirement for some employees, her financial planning team should assist her in closely tracking any targets she may still have, to ensure she doesn't miss out on receiving her equity compensation due to not owning enough shares.

I am sure by now you can appreciate the challenge of retirement planning for Carol. How much to save? Where to save? Is she fully leveraging all benefits offered through her employer? How does she stay on top of all of this and still have time for a career, family, friends, and personal interests?

It becomes a daunting task, and Carol has often felt there were just not enough hours in the day to address it.

Fortunately, Carol's financial planning team is on top of it and can help her navigate the answers to these questions. After all, they have taken the time to fully understand what is important to Carol, Walter, and their family, and they have the knowledge, experience, and tools to help her understand how each benefit fits into the overall plan.

CHAPTER TWELVE

STEP **8**

LONG-TERM CARE PLANNING

ONE OF THE FINAL PIECES for the retirement portion of Carol's financial plan is addressing the risk of her potential need for additional care as she and Walter get older. Whether that need is in the form of in-home care, assisted living, formal nursing home care, or hospice, there is a seventy percent chance[13] that Carol and Walter will need some form of care in the later years of life.

Like the other forms of risk management planning we have discussed, this is not a topic Carol is excited to spend time thinking about. She has visited family members' nursing homes in the past, and the idea of spending her last years of life there is not appealing.

That said, the statistics are pretty clear. A long-term care event is not a financial topic she can afford to ignore without putting the rest of her retirement planning at significant risk. Currently, the average cost of care in a nursing home

---

13   https://longtermcare.acl.gov/the-basics/index.html, "https://longtermcare.acl.gov/the-basics/index.html," [Online]. Available: https://longtermcare.acl.gov/the-basics/index.html. [Accessed 27 11 2017].

in the city Carol lives is approximately $75,000 per year[14,15]. Certainly, this is not insignificant. The data is actually even more sobering. When all long-term care costs are included, an American turning 65 in 2016 will incur $138,000 in future costs, according to the U.S. Department of Health and Human Services[16].

The average length of stay in a nursing home varies, but the financial risk of not planning for a long-term care event could derail all the work and plans she has made. Carol had researched long-term care costs online and figured that in order to consider self-insuring (by using her assets like retirement accounts and the like to pay the expense), she would likely need to have at least $6 million in savings and investment accounts. While she is hopeful to have that much saved one day, she does not feel it would be prudent to assume it will be the case.

Also, like many of our clients, Carol is very concerned about being a burden financially to her children later in life. She has observed the stress that a loved one's deteriorating health has on their adult children, and she does not want to add the stress of asking her children to make tough financial decisions around what assets to spend, sell, or liquidate to cover the costs.

WHAT ABOUT MEDICARE OR MEDICAID?

While they could cover some of the cost, Medicare and Medicaid are likely not options Carol would want to rely on. Therefore, careful long-term care planning is extreme-

---

14   U.S. Department of Health and Services, "www.longtermcare.acl.gov," 21 February 2017. [Online]. Available: https://longtermcare.acl.gov/costs-how-to-pay/costs-of-care.html. [Accessed 20 September 2017].

15   M. LaPonsie, "www.medsave.com," 1 March 2012. [Online]. Available: http://www.medsave.com/articles/Nursing-home-care-averages-almost-90000-a-year.htm. [Accessed 20 September 2017].

16   Melissa Favreault, Urban Institute and Judith Dey, OFFICE OF THE ASSISTANT SECRETARY FOR PLANNING AND EVALUATION, "www.aspe.hhs.gov," February 2016. [Online]. Available: https://aspe.hhs.gov/basic-report/long-term-services-and-supports-older-americans-risks-and-financing-research-brief. [Accessed 20 September 2017].

ly important to help uncover all potential funding options available. The real question is: Will she have the courage to logically look at the facts and take action to address this emotionally touchy topic?

As stated before, it will be important that Carol's financial planning team has access to specialists in the area of long-term care funding options. The solutions available are constantly evolving, and the insurance carriers she chooses should be financially stable. With good advice and emotional courage, Carol will be able to address Step 8 of the Financial Security Checklist and adequately prepare financially for a potential long-term care event.

Our belief is that a retirement plan that has not addressed the risk of a long-term care event is not a plan. It is a hope.

CHAPTER THIRTEEN

STEP 9

EDUCATION FUNDING

NOW THAT CAROL'S RETIREMENT PICTURE is secure, she can move forward with addressing Step 9 on her Financial Security Checklist, funding Ben and Ava's college education.

With tuition costs continuing to increase at a rate double the national inflation rate, this is an intimidating goal for Carol. That said, she and Walter have decided they do not want Ben and Ava to graduate from college carrying the burden of student loan debt, and she is very interested in understanding the options available.

Through her employer, Carol is currently not offered a benefit that assists in planning for her children's college education. For this portion of her planning, then, she will need to explore alternatives outside of her company.

After speaking with her financial planning team, she learns there are several options available. She could simply open a savings or investment account in the children's names. She could open a Coverdell Education IRA. She could utilize an individual investment account. Or she could use a 529 College Savings Plan.

TAX TREATMENT OF A 529

Ultimately, she settles on the option most of our clients utilize, which is a 529 College Savings Plan. The primary advantage to the 529 Plan is the tax structure. When making contributions, the amount she puts into a plan is typically not tax deductible (exceptions depend on the state where she lives and the plan she utilizes). This means that her contributions do not avoid tax when they are made. Once the money is contributed to the account, all the growth and interest from the investments are tax deferred. This means, she will not pay tax each year on the growth and interest. At the point where Ben and Ava are heading off to college, she can use the money to pay for college-related expenses (tuition, room and board, etc.) tax-free.

Her financial advisor will help her assess how best to invest within the 529, based on several factors including her risk appetite, the age of her children, and when the money would be needed.

When Carol and Walter have reached that milestone of parenting and are ready to joyfully (and maybe a bit tearfully) launch Ben and Ava's college journeys, they can do so with the support of their financial planning team. At least financially, they can have confidence that they are well-prepared.

Again, with the constantly changing tax codes and financial products available, Carol will want to work closely with her financial planning team to ensure she is fully aware of the options available to successfully address her goal for Ben and Ava's college. In doing so, she will accomplish Step 9 on her way to financial security: Save for her children's college expenses.

CHAPTER FOURTEEN

DO YOU HAVE A TEAM?

THROUGHOUT THE COURSE of Carol's story and her journey toward becoming financially secure, I have referenced her team. This suggests that Walter and Carol should be working with a financial planning team, instead of one individual advisor.

Why might this be important?

While the saying goes, "Two heads are better than one," in the financial planning world, it is simply not possible for one individual, no matter how talented he or she is, to be an expert in every nuance of the financial planning universe.

Most clients, just like Carol, are not expecting their financial advisor to know every aspect of recent tax law changes, different investment strategies, or the multitude of insurance benefits. What they are expecting is for their advisor to have access to a team of specialists who are experts in these specific areas.

Therefore, as discussed back when Carol was picking a financial advisor, she will want to be sure her advisor has a team behind him or her. This team includes individuals with specialized knowledge and experience, including an estate planning attorney, a CPA, a mortgage broker, and an insurance agent.

Step 10 in a solid financial plan is to develop a team that ensures you are covering all aspects with excellent advice. In today's world, we believe this is the only way to successfully reach financial security.

CHAPTER FIFTEEN

UPDATE REGULARLY

I AM FOND OF SAYING, "Financial planning is NOT a date in time. It is not something you carve in stone once implemented and say it is complete." Clients who have a financial plan like Carol will need to be constantly updating the plan. As she moves into different roles within her company, new or different benefits might be presented. Or her company could simply change the benefits offered. As her family moves through the different stages of life, different needs should be addressed. As we discussed, she will need to focus on her retirement planning first, but once that is secure, then move into planning options for Ben and Ava's college education. And the list goes on.

Carol will want to regularly meet with her financial planning team to update her plan and make sure it is staying on track. This is Step 11: Schedule annual reviews and follow-up meetings. I have met many clients who felt like they had a great plan. Some have even brought the plan into my office and flipped through their leather-bound booklet and glossy pages with pride. Yet, a nice looking plan that sits on the shelf, but is not regularly reviewed and executed, is not worth the paper it is printed on. Personally, I would take a mediocre plan that is well-executed over an amazing plan poorly executed.

Your financial advisor's job does not stop with creating a plan. Believe it or not, creating the plan is the easy part. It is much more difficult to decide when to stick to a plan—despite what markets do, what advice is trending on the internet, or what a coworker does—and when to change a plan because new information is available or because goals have changed. What's most important, then, is: Will your advisor help you modify the plan, when necessary and prudent, and execute the plan?

Bill Hybels says it this way in his book *Axiom: Powerful Leadership Proverbs*, "The nature of human beings is such that we tend not to drift into better behaviors. We usually have to be asked by someone to consider taking it up a level."[17] In regards to your financial plan, your financial advisor should be challenging you to take it up a level.

---

17   B. Hybels, *Axiom: Powerful Leadership Proverbs*, Zondervan, 2011.

CHAPTER SIXTEEN

TAKE ACTION

SO WHY DID I WRITE THIS SHORT LITTLE BOOK? And who are Carol, Walter, Ben, and Ava? If you guessed that these fictional characters are based upon my years of experience working with clients just like them, you are mostly correct. I made up this story to give you a simple, easy-to-follow resource to use as you plan your life using a different perspective and pursue your version of financial security. Understanding your benefits and how to best leverage those benefits is not hard, but many people simply do not know what they do not know. When it comes to their financial planning, this costs them in real dollars and cents. Therefore, I really hope these pages become a catalyst for you to take action.

Maybe, for you, taking action means you start distinguishing between your savings account and your deferred spending account. Maybe it is realizing the importance of insuring against the things you cannot afford to lose. Maybe it is simply realizing you need some help on this journey, not out of lack of understanding or desire to implement and execute a financial plan, but out of lack of time to stay on top of all the details that go into making the most of your resources.

Whatever it is, I challenge and encourage you to take action. Don't delay.

FOR MORE INFORMATION AND TO VIEW TESTIMONIALS FROM CLIENTS, VISIT MY WEBSITE AT WWW.JOSH-WAITE.COM

Bestselling author and leadership consultant, John Maxwell, has a phrase for delaying action in his book, *The 15 Invaluable Laws of Growth*. It is, "The Law of Diminishing Intent." This Law says, "The longer you wait to do something you should do now, the greater the odds that you will never actually do it."[1]

So when I say, "Don't delay," it is because I know that if you put this off, it will be much more likely to slip through the cracks.

Now I need to the answer the question, "Who are Carol, Walter, Ben, and Ava?" While the story is completely made up, the characters represent four of the most important people in my life.

Carol is the name of my grandmother who passed away in 2013. During her time on this earth, she was a constant encourager. And she still encourages me today. You see, The Law of Diminishing Intent almost got the best of me in writing this book. Although I believed in my heart that this book could have tremendous impact, knowing that the main character was chosen in honor of Grandma Carol inspired me to finish it when I was tempted to put it off. Yep,

---

1   J. Maxwell, The 15 Invaluable Laws of Growth, Center Street, 2014.

she's still encouraging me today!

Walter is the name of my father, who passed away in 2004. He will forever be one of my heroes. His desire to help others was unlike anything I have ever seen. At the same time, he was often the one who challenged me to take it up a level. And while he no longer is with us in person, his challenge has never left me, and this book is my way of carrying forward the torch of helping others.

Lastly, Ben and Ava are the names of our two children. Along with my wife, Nikki, they are my inspiration today. They would love me whether I completed this book or not. My desire to be an example for them pushed me to not give up, and my hope is that they never give up on their dreams as well.

Live Life Differently,

Josh Waite
P.S. If you would like to connect with me directly, please email joshwaite@upanddownthemountain.com.

ACKNOWLEDGEMENTS

I WANT TO ACKNOWLEDGE and thank my amazing wife, Nikki, for her unfailing support and encouragement. She has stood by my side through good and bad, and I couldn't imagine going through life without her. I also want to thank my mom for her support and her assistance with proofreading. A retired professor, she has not needed to proof my homework or papers for many years, but she gladly stepped up to do so for this book. Thanks to Amy Stoller for being a great friend and for editing the book and coordinating with Jocelyn Baker to get it published. And special thanks to one of my business partners Shawn Mazander for reviewing content and giving his valuable input. And of course, all thanks are due to God, who enables me to live life differently. Romans 8:28

ABOUT THE AUTHOR

JOSHUA T. WAITE, CFP®, CLU®, ChFC®, CAP®, is a Wealth Management Advisor and the Managing Director of the Northwestern Mutual-Greater Peoria organization. His mission is to help those he leads, who are often Fortune 500 executives, to live life differently. As a Wealth Management Advisor, he has helped thousands of individuals live life differently through charting a course to financial security.

In this book, he will share how his experience climbing Mount Rainier in 2014 showed him the many correlations between climbing a mountain and the work he does every day with the clients he serves. To successfully scale a mountain, you need a good map and a guide with expertise and perspective to get you to the summit—and safely down again. Josh also tells of his experiences helping Fortune 500 executives develop their plans to successfully climb the mountain of complex financial products and ever-changing compensation packages to achieve their summit of financial security, and to enjoy a safe journey down the mountain of retirement.

Josh is a graduate of Bradley University with a degree in finance. He is active in the community serving on several local boards, and he believes that faith and family come first in life. He and his wife, Nikki, have two children, Ben and Ava, and make their home in Peoria, Illinois.

Made in the USA
Columbia, SC
19 February 2019